Spell
Spinners

'Spell Spinners'
An original concept by Cath Jones
© Cath Jones 2023

Illustrated by Amanda Erb

Published by MAVERICK ARTS PUBLISHING LTD
Studio 11, City Business Centre, 6 Brighton Road,
Horsham, West Sussex, RH13 5BB
© Maverick Arts Publishing Limited May 2023
+44 (0)1403 256941

ISBN 978-1-84886-964-6

Maverick
publishing

www.maverickbooks.co.uk

White

This book is rated as: White Band (Guided Reading)

Spell Spinners

By Cath Jones

Illustrated by Amanda Erb

Chapter 1

Miranda Harkfright hopped onto her broomstick and zoomed out of the dormitory window.

The other trainee witches were already lined up outside the Keep Fit classroom. Miranda landed just as the door burst open.

"Welcome to hula hooping!" boomed their teacher, Lavender McTaff. "Please leave your broomsticks and wands in the porch. Remember, Keep Fit is a magic-free zone!"

Miranda's heart thumped with excitement as she added her broomstick to the pile. She couldn't wait to have a go at hula hooping. Miranda popped her magic wand into a large pot and hurried into the room, spotting Holly Leech at the front by the hula hoops.

Lavender handed a sparkling hula hoop to each of the witches.

"First, we will spin the hoop on our hips," she said. Within seconds, the room whizzed with spinning hoops. But Miranda's hula hoop simply flopped to the floor.

"Next, we will spin the hoop on our wrists and arms," Lavender said.

Miranda concentrated really hard as she windmilled her arms. But her hula hoop shot into the air, bounced off the ceiling and flew across the room.

"Watch it!" shrieked Holly.

Miranda sighed as she watched Holly spin her hoop. She made it look so easy!

"Our third spin will be around our necks," Lavender announced.

Once again, Miranda failed completely. Why was she the only one who couldn't do this? Her eyes filled with tears of frustration.

At the end of the session, all the trainee witches filed out of the classroom. But something made Miranda look back.

Holly was standing at the back of the room, smirking. She had a magic wand in her hand!

Miranda stumbled out into the sunshine, her mind whirling with questions. Could her hoop have been bewitched by Holly?

Chapter 2

Miranda flew up into the clouds. She needed to be alone to think about what had just happened.

She closed her eyes for a moment and pictured the porch and the classroom.

She didn't remember seeing Holly put her wand in the pot in the porch. Holly must have used magic during Keep Fit. She was a hula hoop cheat!

Slowly, a plan began to form in Miranda's mind. If she wanted to outwit Holly, she'd have to break the rules too.

Back in the dormitory, Miranda pulled out her spell book. She turned the pages, hunting for a suitable spinning spell. There was only one that looked easy enough. She spent the week memorising it until, finally, it was time for Keep Fit.

Miranda made sure to stand right at the front of the classroom, close to the stack of hula hoops. As Lavender prepared to hand them out, Miranda closed her eyes and began to mutter the long spinning spell. She was almost finished when there was a loud shout.

"Hey! What are you up to?" Holly demanded.

Miranda's eyes flew open. Instantly, the rest of the spell vanished from her mind!

HISS! SWIP! WHOOSH!

The unfinished spell hissed into the air, zinged round the room and hit the pile of hula hoops. Miranda knew that her spell was invisible to other witches, but she couldn't help glancing around anxiously.

Holly looked at her suspiciously.

Miranda ignored Holly as she took a hoop from Lavender. Would her unfinished spell work? She gulped nervously as she began to spin the hoop.

It spun beautifully!

Throughout the session, all the witches twirled their hoops like experts.

"Marvellous! Fabulous! Fantastic!" Lavender cooed. "Best hula hooping I've ever seen!"

Miranda glowed with pride. Her spell had worked!

Chapter 3

By bedtime, Miranda began to wonder whether her spinning spell was too good! All day long, witches had been hula hooping in all their lessons! They'd even started to spin their spell books and wands.

By supper time the next day, Miranda was certain something was seriously wrong. A kind of spinning madness had spread throughout school.

She watched in alarm as a cat trotted across the lawn and then, **WHOOSH!** It began to spin round and round. Birds flew in circles and even the gardener's mowing looked circular.

Whenever anyone spun a hula hoop, everything nearby began to spin too. The unfinished spell's magic seemed to be getting stronger!

Miranda tiptoed into the dining hall, nervously checking for hula-hoopers.

"Phew!" She was alone. But just as she sat down, a spiral of hula-hooping witches spun into the dining hall. "Eeek!" Miranda ducked beneath a table.

But Holly was already hiding there! "You're safe here," said Holly, "as long as the tables don't start spinning!"

Miranda froze. She stared speechlessly at Holly.

"It's odd how everything has started to spin since Keep Fit..." Holly continued.

"Oh, um, yes," Miranda agreed.

Together they sat and watched the hula-hooping witches. They seemed to be bewitching everything in the room. The soup began to bubble and froth. The trifle bulged alarmingly. A wave of mashed potato soared around the room! Food whizzed round and round.

Soon, the dining hall was a spinning, splattering mess. Nothing was safe from Miranda's spinning spell!

Suddenly, a sausage spun under the table. It whacked Miranda on the nose.

"Ow!" she squealed. Then she leapt up and fled. 'I have to find a way of reversing my unfinished spell,' she thought.

Chapter 4

Desperately, Miranda searched her spell book. There had to be a way to reverse the unfinished spell...

Nothing! Perhaps the witches' ancient spell book could help?

It was pitch dark in the library. Miranda crept slowly towards the bookshelves. Suddenly, out of the darkness, a voice boomed, "What are you doing?"

Miranda shrieked in alarm as Holly stepped out of the shadows.

"You're behind all this crazy spinning, aren't you?!" Holly accused her.

Miranda hesitated before finally admitting. "But only because you used magic on me first. If you hadn't put a spell on my hula hoop, none of this would've happened…"

Holly looked shocked. "It was just a bit of fun. I was only mucking around..."

"It wasn't fun!" interrupted Miranda. "You made me feel miserable!"

"Oh." Holly gazed at the ground for a moment. "Sorry..." she muttered. Miranda sighed.

"Are you looking for an anti-spinning spell?" Holly asked. Miranda nodded.

"I've already looked," Holly said. "There's nothing here. You'll have to invent a spell."

"But I'm only a trainee witch. No trainee could do that without help..." Miranda said.

"I know. No trainee could do it *alone*," Holly said.

Miranda glanced at Holly. "Should I ask Professor Lavender for help?" she asked.

Holly shook her head. A smile spread across her face. "We could work together..."

Miranda looked thoughtful. She couldn't invent a spell on her own. Perhaps Holly was right. Should they work together?

"After all," Holly added, "*we* created this mess!"

Slowly, Miranda nodded in agreement.

Chapter 5

Miranda and Holly collapsed onto the floor. They'd been working on an anti-spinning spell for hours. Miranda yawned and held out a piece of paper.

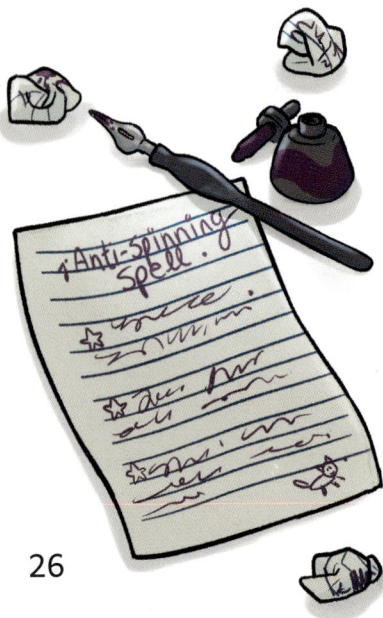

Holly read the short spell and frowned. "The only way we'll know for sure whether it works is if we try it..."

Miranda nodded.

"Are you sure you can remember the right way to wave your wand?" Holly asked.

"Don't worry," Miranda flicked her wand delicately in the air. "See!"

The two girls set off to find some hula-hooping witches. But the dormitory was empty, as was the dining hall, so they headed into the garden.

Miranda's hair fluttered in a gentle breeze. Suddenly, she spotted Lavender at the head of a spinning whirl of witches.

"Ready?" Holly asked.

"Let's do this!" Miranda answered.

Holly pulled out the spell and began to chant. Miranda aimed her wand but, suddenly, the gentle breeze began to spin!

"Tornado!" Holly yelled.

The witches looked round in alarm, but it was too late. The tornado sucked them straight up into the air!

Miranda and Holly yelled their spell and twirled their wands. The spell travelled up the tornado like a flash of lightning. In an instant, the tornado vanished. The witches tumbled down onto the grass.

The pile of witches began to cheer. "Hooray for Miranda and Holly. They saved us from the tornado."

But Lavender frowned. "How did you two know how to cast an anti-spinning spell?" she asked.

Miranda blushed.

"It's my fault," Holly blurted out.

"No, it's my fault," Miranda said.

"You can explain in my office," Lavender said in a grim voice.

★ ★ ★

Miranda and Holly spent the next week cleaning up the mess they'd caused. Lavender had been impressed with their spell making but not their rule breaking.

As they scrubbed, Holly grinned. "We make a great team."

Miranda laughed. "We do, and it's much more fun being best friends than mortal enemies. But just wait till I beat you at hula hooping next week," she winked.

"Ha, you mean until I beat *you!*" said Holly.

"You're on!"

The End

Book Bands for Guided Reading

The colour labels on the left, top to bottom:

Pink

Red

Yellow

Blue

Green

Orange

Turquoise

Purple

Gold

White

The Institute of Education book banding system is a scale of colours that reflects the various levels of reading difficulty. The bands are assigned by taking into account the content, the language style, the layout and phonics. Word, phrase and sentence level work is also taken into consideration.

Maverick Early Readers are a bright, attractive range of books covering the pink to white bands. All of these books have been book banded for guided reading to the industry standard and edited by a leading educational consultant.

Early Reader — Cool Duck and Lots of Hats
By Elizabeth Dale

Early Reader — Catch It, Jess! and Cat Nap
by Katie Dale, Illustrated by Kassia Dudziuk

Early Reader — The Space Race
by Jenny Jinks, Illustrated by Serena Lombardo

Early Reader — Pirates Don't Drive Diggers
by Alex English, Illustrated by Duncan Beedie

Early Reader — A Right Royal Mess

To view the whole Maverick Readers scheme, visit our website at www.maverickearlyreaders.com

Or scan the QR code above view our scheme instantl